# A Bryant Family History

By

Victoria London Gladden

# PREFACE

From the moment we are born, time is at once all that we have and the one thing we never have enough of. The alpha and the omega of our existence here on earth. We start our lives at a crawl and spend the majority of our childhood wishing we could be older. That way we may fully experience the life that is ahead of us and be free from the incumbrances of our Parents. Little do we know that as we move gradually from a crawl to a walk then rapidly forward our lives will accelerate to speeds we never thought possible. Ever looking forward to what lies ahead, not worrying about the little things that we will one day find to be so important. After all, we have all the time we need, right? Where are we going? How and when will we arrive?

The excitement of life is exhilarating. As we speed along we begin to chronicle our time here with photos, letters, postcards, newspaper clippings and stories passed along by family and loved ones. As time goes by, we eventually begin to wonder not so much about where we are going but where we have been. Where did I come from? We then return to the photo albums, boxes and dresser drawers filled with memories struck in time. All of those moments that made our life what it is today. Mothers, Fathers, Grand Parents, Aunts and Uncles, Cousins and countless family and friends that stare back at us from a time gone by. As we gaze at that split second in time, that photograph tells a story all its own. The story is much larger and longer than the time it took to capture it. All we have to do is look closely.

In the following pages are moments frozen in time of the family of Thomas Reid and Margaret Bryant. It is and was with great love and care that the photos here were kept in the hopes that they can be shared with family members still with us and those that are yet to come. Every effort has been made to make sure that names and places are correct to the best of our knowledge. The hope is that you enjoy seeing these images and are filled with a sense of pride for being a part of the Bryant Family Tree.

Enjoy,

Jefferson Reid Gladden

The Bryant Family

# The Bryant Family

This is about the Bryant Family from Alabama. We will begin as far back as the photos take us.  The images were in the collection of Mildred (Mit) Bryant and have been passed down through the family. Mildred Beatrice Bryant is the youngest of the 11 children born to Thomas Reid and Margaret Marilla Andrews Bryant.  I am married to a Bryant descendant, Jefferson Reid Gladden. He is the last grandchild born of Thomas Reid Bryant and Margaret Andrews Bryant. That is the direct line we are following.

Thanks goes to Anita Gladden Smith and to my husband Jeff for all the help going through boxes and files to get this information together. Every effort has been taken to give you the correct information as it was passed on.  If you don't see your photo in the book, please know that I did the best I could to get every family represented if possible. My goal is to preserve the history of the family so these photos are not lost or tossed in a drawer through the years. They should be shared and not just in a box in the collection of Mit's family. Here is the Bryant Family in pictures. The main family members from just a few generations back start the story.

Some may have traced the family back further but we will start with Colman James Bryant (1819-1880). He was one of six children born to William Franklin Bryant (1790-1864) and Delilah Dillard (1796-1875). Colman married Elezene Cohen (1825-1870) pictured below. The spelling for their names came from their tombstones. There seems to be lots of different spellings for a lot of family names.  They had 12 children, including William Franklin Bryant (1853-1941) who is in the direct line.  We will start with William Franklin and Julia Ann Hardwick Bryant on the next page and move through history in pictures.

Elezene Cohen Bryant

Colman James Bryant

Mr. & Mrs. W. F. Bryant in 1897 in Hebron, AL.

Pictured here are William Franklin Bryant (Dec. 27,1853-Nov. 11, 1941) and Julia Ann Hardwick Bryant (May 13, 1857-April 4, 1950). This is where the photos begin to come to life.

# William Franklin Bryant married Julia Ann Hardwick on Sept. 18,1875.

## He was twenty-one and she was just eighteen.

### They had 10 children.

Thomas Reid (Oct.1,1876-Oct. 4,1969) or <u>T.R.</u>
Lawrence David (Oct. 1,1878-Dec.11,1962)
Walter Gray (Nov. 3,1880-Sept.11,1959)
Benjamin Hill (April 13,1883-Jan 22,1972) or <u>B.H.</u>
Lola Dee (August 27,1885-Dec.25,1989)
Nola Edna (Nov. 16,1888-Oct. 9,1973)
Henry Harris ( April 16,1890-Jan.5,1957)
William Homer (Feb.7,1893-March 7,1983)
Curtis Hardwick (Sept.22,1895-Jan.2,1997)
Julia Bessie (Sept.3,1897-Nov.13,1982)

I underlined the name that was most written on the photographs when they were labeled. I believe that is the name that they used most often.

I knew there was talk of the long lives of the family members, but notice that Curtis lived to be 101. But hold on! Lola lived to be 104. That is a long life. Oh, the stories they could tell if they were still here with us. Take time to talk to those who have lived long lives before they are gone. We must preserve the history of our families.

As I did the research, I was always looking for the birth and death dates of the ancestors. It doesn't take much to realize that is not what is the most important about a person.  It is that time between birth and death that makes us who we are. And more important is what you do with that time.  You want people to remember you for what you did with your life between birth and death. Make the most of the day that was given you. Life is short. Live each day as if it is your last.

# Home Sweet Home for the Bryant Family

This is William and Julia Bryant's first home in Hebron.

We will begin here in Hebron, Alabama. Pictured here are L-R: Thomas Reid, Lola, William Franklin, Henry, Nola, Julia holding Homer. Back L-R: Walter, Lawrence, Ben. They were often known by their two initials.  Ben was often called B.H. for Benjamin Hill Bryant. Since Homer was a baby, the photo must have been taken around 1894. There would be two more children born by 1897 and a few years after that they would be in a new and bigger home to fit them all in.

William Franklin Bryant was later known to the family as "Will Dad" and Julia Ann Bryant was "Julie Mam". This is the family in front of their 2nd home in Hebron, Alabama in 1900. I am not sure about the folks on the porch posing so pretty but here are the ones that I think are Bryant Family according to the names written on the back. L-R: Andrew held by Thomas Reid, Ethel in front of her Dad, Margaret, Henry, Curtis, Nola, Walter, Lola, Ben, and Lawrence. In front are Homer, Julie Mam, Bessie and Will Dad.

Julia Ann Hardwick Bryant was the daughter of James Hardwick and Melitha Bollinger Hardwick. James Hardwick (1823-Sept.20,1863) was thought to be killed in the battle of Chickamauga in the Civil War and is buried in that cemetery. I have not found a record of that as of yet except in notes left by the family. A lot of the soldiers killed do not have a marked grave. Melitha (Dec.6,1821-1862) would die before James so that would leave the children as orphans.  They have not been found living with relatives in any census checked yet. That is a question to answer.  Who raised the children after their Mom and Dad had died. Maybe you know the answer. I could not find the answer in my research.

Another photo of the house in Hebron. Must be a few years later because of the landscape there now. No dates or names were on the photograph. They seem to always be dressed in their Sunday clothes for the camera.

Many stories have been told about the Bryant family and what a wonderful family they were and continue to be.  One of William and Julia's sons, Walter, wrote it best in 1931. "Their lives are an inspiration to us all. So, you see that it was not money that prompted Dad and Mother to keep on working for us, it was faith in God and the hope that some or all of us would be a blessing to them and our fellow man and Country." What an honor to have that written about your family.

On the back of the photo it reads: The last home that Will Dad built in Wellington. Still standing and occupied. I am not sure what year that was written but I understand that it has been torn down now. Walter Bryant wrote about his father in 1931, "When he needed a new house he just went to the woods, cut his timber and cleared up another new ground and got more fresh land and a new house all at the same time, like the one he built in 1875, another in 1882 and another in 1900 that us older boys helped build."  Today Johnny Reid Bryant, a great grandson, owns the property close to the old home place. A lot of the Bryant family has stayed close to that area in Alabama.

Front: Will Dad and Julie Mam. Back L-R: Lawrence, Henry, Nola, Homer, Bess, Lola, Curtis, B.H., Thomas Reid, and Walter. That is all 10 of the Bryant children.

This is the W.F. Bryant Home in Wellington, Alabama again. If you look closely, you can see someone on the stairs with what looks like a Doctors bag. Makes you wonder what was going on that day at the Bryant Home.  Everyone is moving about but seem aware that a picture is being taken. Maybe a new member of the family had just been born? I hope that no one was ill? Only they know for sure.

This is the same house and the same day it seems but everyone is in the picture now.  I do not have the names of all the children and grandchildren present but 10 has grown into many more.  It looks like lots of grandchildren have joined the family. I am missing a lot of photos between this one and the later years. They are probably in a drawer somewhere waiting to be rediscovered.  Share while you know who is who.  Always write names and dates on the photos for loved ones later because someone will wonder who they are and when the photo was taken just like we are doing here today.

# Children of William Franklin and Julia Ann Bryant

Now the photographs will show the family members and some of their children. I don't have information on all the siblings but this will give you some insight into their lives.  This is the second son of William Franklin and Julia Bryant. Lawrence was born just after Thomas Reid. There is much more about T.R. later since he is the direct line.

Here are Lawrence (1878-1962), Wallace (1884-1958) his wife and the two children they had at the time. The photos must have been taken before 1916 when Susie Mae joined the family. They must have taken Gladys and Cecil Bryant to the same photographer who used the same background year after year. If it works, don't change it. Lawrence and Wallace had three children, Cecil, Gladys and Susie May. Susie May is not pictured.

Nola Bryant Line (1887-1973) and one of her children are in the top photo. Nola and Samuel Line had three children, two boys and a girl.  On the right is Bessie Bryant (1897-1982). She married Buford Cartledge. They did not have any children.

Thomas Reid, the oldest child, on the left in his hat, and Curtis Hardwick Bryant (1895-1997) in his Military uniform is pictured in the right bottom photo. He was in the service from December 13,1917 -February 17,1920.  He made it through World War I and lived a long life. He was 101 when he passed away in 1997.  A lot of the Bryant family members lived long lives. Lola, pictured on the next page, lived to be 104. Yes 104.

# Children of William Franklin and Julia Ann Bryant

On the left is Lola Dee Bryant (1885-1989). She and her husband James Aderholdt had five children.  This is Ferrol Aderholdt, their son on the right.  Lola and Jim owned and operated a Mill in North Alabama by the side of the Little Tallaseehatchee Creek. It was built in 1835 and was one of the first grist mills in Alabama. It was still being run in 1976 by Jim Aderholdt when he died at 94. It was added to the U.S. Historical Register of Historic Places in 1988. It was sold in 1995 and turned into a home and is still a residence today.

Ferrol Aderholdt grew up to be a craftsman and woodworker in the Jacksonville, Alabama area. He made many an alter for the churches in that area along with furniture and restoration of pieces that needed to be saved. James and Lola had five children but Ferrol is the only one that I have information about.  He even had an article in the paper about his work as a craftsman so he must have been very talented.

Thomas Reid is our direct line that we are following in this journey. Here is a tintype photo of Thomas Reid Bryant (1876-1969) that was found in Mildred Bryant's things after she passed away. On the back of the photo was written: "Papa T.R. Bryant" but no year was indicated. It has to be in his early years.

These are much later photographs of Curtis Bryant and his family. You know the Christmas Cards with photos people like to send out every year to friends and family. You may wonder what people do with those after the holidays are over. We know what Mildred Bryant did with them. She kept those, even from the 1940s. They were very special to her. This is 10 Christmas photos from Curtis Bryant and his family that were sent to Mit. Curtis married Mildred Crusselle in 1940 and they had three children. Here is a peek into their life during that time in photographs. Pictured are Curtis, Mildred, Bonnie, Marticia, Curtis Jr. and Jera the dog.  What a wonderful collection of memories.

The Curtis Hardwick Bryant Family in Christmas photos sent every year. What a lovely family. Curtis worked in the Insurance Business so he may have mailed these out to his clients. We know Mildred Bryant kept these as precious photos of the family. I am glad she did.

This is just as the picture reads. The Reid Bryant Family. No names were listed on this one other than what is on the front. If I looked long enough, I am sure I could get the names right but I will leave that to you. There is the porch swing that seems to have been there for many years but we are not sure the location. From 1920 to the present is a long time to be getting together for reunions. There are ten children and it seems there may be grandchildren in the picture as well. No one had labeled the photo so we can only guess.

# William Franklin Bryant and Julia Hardwick Bryant

Noccalula Falls must have been a tourist spot even in those days.

Will Dad and Julie Mam or better known as William Franklin and Julia Bryant.

The couple, William Franklin and Julia Bryant in 1923. Why are they in Decatur, GA? I do not have the answer to that question. They are all dressed up for something.  I hope it was a special occasion.  Walter, their son, had a furniture store in Decatur, GA. Maybe they went to visit.

This is John Bryant and his son Leslie. They seemed dressed up for something also.  Look closely at the photos. Do John and William look alike to you? They should because they are brothers.

A Bryant Family Reunion years later. Everyone is grown with children and even grandchildren. Below is a picture of Hazel, Lola, Will Dad and Julie Mam as they called her.  Remember Lola lived to be 104 so she was around for lots of reunions.

Top left photo is of Bessie, Lola, Julie Mam, and Nola. On the right is Uncle Walter and Aunt Exa. The bottom photo includes Ethel, Thomas Reid, Helen, Will Dad and Julie Mam. Maybe at another reunion?

I am sure there were photos in between the years but these were the next ones that Mit had in her collection. This is a group of those that attended the 50th Wedding Anniversary Celebration of William and Julia Bryant.  There were no names on the photo. It looks like a large celebration with lots of family there.

September 16, 1925 was their 50th Wedding Anniversary. They had the celebration at Sulphur Springs, Alabama. They were married in September of 1875. Pictured below are John Bryant, Joshua Bryant, William and Julia. John and Joshua are brothers to William Bryant.

It's the Family Reunion of 1928 and looks like all the family is here. L-R: William Franklin, Julia, then in line by birth order, Thomas Reid, Lawrence, Walter, Ben, Lola, Nola, Henry, Homer, Curtis, and Bessie.

The photo below has written on it, 1928 Sulphur Springs. All seven of the Brothers are pictured here. L-R: Thomas Reid, Lawrence, Walter, Ben., Henry, Homer, and Curtis. It was probably the same day as the top photo.

This is Mr. & Mrs. William Bryant and all of the Bryant children on their 56th Wedding Anniversary Celebration, September 16th, 1931 in Wellington, AL.  Pictured are L-R: Curtis Hardwick, William Homer, Henry Harris, Benjamin Hill, Walter Gray, Lawrence David, Thomas Reid, William Franklin, Julia Hardwick Bryant, Lola Dee, Nola Edna and Julia Bessie. Below is a photo of Will Dad and Julie Mam.

Pictured above are Mr. and Mrs. W. F. Bryant, who celebrated their 63rd wedding anniversary at their home at Wellington Friday. Mr. Bryant is 84 and Mrs. Bryant is 81. Both are natives of this county and are members of families first to settle here. Before her marriage, Mrs. Bryant was Miss Julia Hardwick. Both are in good health. They have 10 children, all of them living. They are T. R. Bryant of Cedar Springs, L. D. Bryant of Wellington, W. G. Bryant of Decatur, Ga., B. H. Bryant of Gadsden, H. H. Bryant of Wellington, W. H. Bryant of Anniston, C. H. Bryant of Atlanta, Mrs. J. J. Aderholdt of near Jacksonville, Mrs. S. W. Line and Mrs. B. N. Cartlidge, both of Gadsden.

A few years later and they make the paper. Here is a copy of the article that was in the paper about their 63 years together. He was 84 at the time. He died at age 88. She was 81 and lived on to be 93. I am sure there were more celebrations but I do not have any photos of those. Share them if you do.

The top photo shows some of her boys with Julie Mam. L-R: Homer, Curtis, Julie Mam, Henry and Thomas Reid. At 92, Julia Bryant could use a rifle with the best of them. Here she is with her catch of the day. Looks like she is having rabbit for dinner. Julie Mam on the right in a field of flowers.  She was 93 when she passed away.

Julia Ann Hardwick Bryant lived May 13,1857-April 4,1950.

What a sweet and lovely woman she was said to be. She lived a long life.

**We are following the Thomas Reid direct line. He was the oldest of William Franklin and Julia Bryant's children.**

## Thomas Reid Bryant married

## Margaret (Maggie) Marilla Andrews

## on October 25, 1896.

# Children of Thomas Reid Bryant

**October 1,1876-October 4, 1969**

# and Margaret Marilla Andrews Bryant

**September 14, 1877-November 1, 1953**

They had eleven children:

Nannie Ethel (April 2,1898-Dec.21,1975)
Andrew Jackson (March 15,1900-Oct. 30,1980)
Effie Elzora (Sept.9,1901-Jan.17,1943)
Anna Mae (May 21,1903-Feb.15,1940)
Thomas Reid Jr. (April 3,1905-July 19,1907)
John Renfroe (Aug.23,1907-Sept. 11,1975)
Velma Odell (Dec.7,1909-Feb. 5,1910)
Clarence Julian (Jan.2,1911-Dec.2,2003)
Ralph Gray (June 29,1913-Dec.4,1983)
Edwin Claxton (May 1,1916-Nov.1,1980)
Mildred Beatrice (July 28,1920-April 28,2011)

# The Thomas Reid Bryant Family

This is the Thomas Reid Bryant Family about 1906.  L-R: Andrew, Thomas Reid Sr. holding Thomas Reid Jr, Elzora, Anna, Margaret Andrews Bryant and Ethel. This is only the beginning for the family. They would have 11 children by 1920. Thomas Reid Bryant Jr. pictured here would only live from April 3,1905 to July 19, 1907. This is the only picture of him that I have and know of.  Velma Odell Bryant who is not yet born when this picture was taken, would only live from Dec. 7,1909 to Feb. 5,1910. The rest would live on to adulthood. Born in 1907-Renfroe, Velma-1909, Clarence-1911, Ralph-1913, Edd-1916, and Mildred-1920.

# The Prickett School in 1909

Here are some of the children at the Prickett School House with Mr. Jack Young as the teacher in 1909. Some of the Bryant children are included. Andrew, Ethel, Elzora and Anna Mae Bryant are in the photo. If you look closely someone has written the names by them. Look even closer and notice that most of them were not wearing shoes.  You are not allowed to go into a school without shoes today. Things have changed so much since 1909.

DILIGENCE LEADS TO VICTORY

# Exchange Report Card

_District No. 21_
Name of School

_Elzora Bryant_
Name of Pupil

_6th_ Grade

For Term Beginning _Jany_

and Ending _Apr. 15, 1915_

_T. R. Bryant_ Teacher

## TO PARENTS

Please examine this report carefully each time presented you, and if not satisfactory, call upon the Superintendent or Principal of the school, and see if some plan may not be devised by which it may be made better. If it is good, speak a kind word of praise to the pupil, and of commendation to the teacher.

### PARENT'S SIGNATURE.

First Month

Second Month

Third Month _T. R. Bryant_

Fourth Month

Fifth Month

Sixth Month

Seventh Month

Eighth Month

Ninth Month

| | 1st Month | 2nd Month | 3rd Month | 4th Month | 5th Month | 6th Month | 7th Month | 8th Month | 9th Month | Averages |
|---|---|---|---|---|---|---|---|---|---|---|
| Days Present | | | | | | | | | | |
| Days Absent | | | | | | | | | | |
| Times Tardy | | | | | | | | | | |
| Deportment | | | 84 | | | | | | | |
| Spelling | | | 97 | | | | | | | |
| Reading | | | 94 | | | | | | | |
| Writing | | | 94 | | | | | | | |
| Arithmetic | | | 88 | | | | | | | |
| Geography | | | 95 | | | | | | | |
| Language | | | 96 | | | | | | | |
| Grammar | | | | | | | | | | |
| Physiology | | | 90 | | | | | | | |
| U. S. History | | | | | | | | | | |
| State History | | | | | | | | | | |
| Civil Gov't. | | | | | | | | | | |
| Agriculture | | | | | | | | | | |
| Music | | | | | | | | | | |
| Drawing | | | | | | | | | | |
| Rhetoric | | | | | | | | | | |
| Algebra | | | | | | | | | | |
| Geometry | | | | | | | | | | |
| Physics | | | | | | | | | | |
| Latin | | | | | | | | | | |
| AVERAGES | | | 90+ | | | | | | | |

Excellent, 90 to 100, E.; Good, 80 to 90, G.; Satisfactory, 70 to 80, S.; Not Satisfactory, 60 to 70, N.; Poor, below 60, P.

### PROMOTION

This Certifies, That the pupil named in this report is promoted

to ___________________________ Grade

____________________ 19______

____________________ Principal

Here is proof that Elzora Bryant did well in school. This is her 6th grade report card. Looks like someone was trying to change some grades though?  She got a 90+ so she should have been ok.  T. R. Bryant signed it so she must have been fine and there was no need for punishment.  Maybe she just saved the good one. The date reads 1915 and I am amazed that it has been saved since 1915.

Here are the Thomas Bryant Family Members about 1923. Back: Clarence and Ralph. Middle L-R are Elzora, her husband Bob Wynn, Ethel and her daughter Ruth, Ethel's husband Cleve Fite, and Renfroe. Front L-R:  Edd, Thomas Reid, Mildred, Margaret and Anna. They spelled Edwin's name Edd on all the writings. The only one missing is Andrew and nothing is indicated on the photo about why he was missing. He would have been 23 by this time so may have been off working by then.  Two of the children had died by this time, Thomas Reid Jr. and Velma Odell Bryant. This photo includes the children plus two husbands and the first-born grandchild Ruth.

# School Days at the Prickett School

The Prickett School with teacher Maude Harrison (far right).

Front L-R: Elzora Bryant, Annie Lee Collum, Zula Prickett, Clarine Duggan, Anna Mae Bryant, Fannie Lou Prickett, Clyde Brittain, Ellen Bryant. Second Row L-R: Dora Bryant, Ethel Bryant, Vernor Bryant, Bessie Bryant, Unknown, Newman Prickett, Unknown, Olen Usrey, Curtis Bryant, Herman Rudd. Third row middle: Andrew Bryant, Curt Prickett, Unknown. Fourth Row L-R: Unknown, Lillian Vice, Willie Prickett, Maggie Vice, Edd Vice, Rayan Prickett, Grover Pickett, Dalton Prickett, Leslie Bryant, Homer Bryant and Earl Alverson. These are the names that were on the back of the photograph. I have given every effort to pass on the information as correctly as possible.

This photo includes a majority of the Bryant children from two generations. There are some other Bryant family members that I am sure are cousins or kin as we say down south. Time has not allowed me to make all the connections but after all, we are all related somehow!

The property where the Prickett School was located is now owned by David Bryant, a great great grandson of Thomas Reid Bryant. He is the great grandson of Renfroe Bryant and grandson of Johnny Reid Bryant.

# The Children of Thomas Reid and Maggie Bryant

Years later, here are some photos of Thomas Reid and Maggie's children as they grew up. This is Ethel Bryant in both photos. Nannie Ethel Bryant Fite was her full name and she was the first born. She lived April 2,1898-December 21,1975. She married Cleve Fite and they had two children, Ruth and Helen. Cleve and Ethel are buried in the Edgemont Cemetery in Anniston, Alabama.

The second child born to Thomas Reid and Maggie Bryant is Andrew Jackson Bryant. He is pictured here and lived March 15,1900-October 30,1980. Andrew married Nannie Clark and they had one child, Harlan. Andrew and Nannie are buried at Union United Methodist Church Cemetery in Wellington, Alabama.

Anna Mae and Elzora were only two years apart and in the above picture they are posing together in a location unknown. In the lower photos are Anna Mae at age 19 and Elzora at age 40. She died two years after this photo was made. She was only 42. Anna Mae died at age 37 so they both died young.

Elzora married Robert Wynn and they had three children, Margaret and Howard and also Bobby Ralph Wynn who was born and died in 1932.

Anna Mae married Ed Moore and they had five children, Edna, Haskell, William Norman (1929-1933) Marlene and Barbara. Ed was the Principal at Cedar Springs School where their children and many of the Bryant children attended.

# Cedar Springs School

Cedar Springs was the school that was attended by many of the Bryant children. Of course, that is because Thomas Reid and Lawson Andrews, Maggie Andrews brother, donated the land for the school to be built on. It was right across the street from T.R. Bryant's house. An easy walk to school each day.

Here we have Renfroe Bryant front and center with the basketball. The 1927 Cedar Springs Basketball team members were front L-R: Claude Andrews, Drennen McGinnis, Renfroe Bryant, Wavel Couch, Johnny Andrews. Second Row: Raymond McGinnis and Aldridge Harvey.

Renfroe Bryant (1907-1975) was the sixth born of the Bryant children. He married Annie Wynn and they had ten children. They are Morris, Edith, Faye, Arlene, Johnny Reid, Charles, Duane, Ernie, Donald and Mickey.

Clarence Bryant (1911-2003) is the eighth child to be born. He married Robbie and they had three children, Billy, Melda and Donnie. Clarence is pictured later in the book.

# Cedar Springs School

School days for Mildred (Mit) and Edd.  Mildred is on the second row and the second in line and Edd is at the end of row two.  Here they are as they got older. Ralph lived June 29,1913-Dec.4,1983. He had six children. Edd lived May 1,1916-November 1, 1980. He married Gwinell and had one child, Belita. Mit lived July 28,1920-April 28, 2011. She married Curtis Gladden and had four children, Terry, Anita, Coleman and Jefferson.

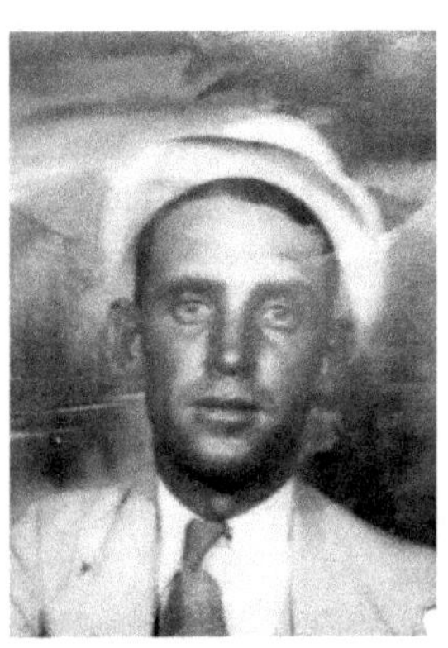

Elzora Bryant Wynn gets the prize for being the best dressed while milking a cow.  On the photo is written Glencoe 1936.  Maybe she just needed milk and did not have time to change. Maybe they always dressed up to milk the cows?  If you look close, you can see a rooster or a hen in the background watching over the situation.  I don't know how to milk a cow and I can't tell if it is a rooster or a hen so I will let you decide that for yourself.

The top photo is Edd Bryant with the Studebaker. It is a 1934 model and the photo was made in 1938. I am not sure who's it was but it was a nice one.  Below are all the brothers. L-R: Edd, Ralph, Clarence, Renfroe, and Andrew in 1947.

More reunions and more photos. The top photo contains five generations of Bryant family members. L-R: Julia Hardwick Bryant, Thomas Reid Bryant, Andrew Bryant, Harlan Bryant and his newborn son Andy. The bottom photo includes some of the children of Maggie and Thomas Reid. L-R: Mildred, Edd, Ralph, Clarence, Renfroe, Andrew, Ethel, and Thomas Reid.

# The Andrews side of the family

We have talked about the Bryant family but there is another side to the family. Margaret Marilla Andrews Bryant was an Andrews before she was a Bryant. She was born on Sept 14, 1877 and died November 1,1953. She was one of 10 children of Hester (Feb. 13,1842-May 1,1890) and Elsberry Jackson Andrews (Oct. 13, 1843-Feb. 28, 1917).  After Hester died in 1890, Elsberry married again in 1894 and had two more children with Lou Gwin.  That makes twelve children to feed. Here is the Andrews side of the story in pictures.

Elsberry Andrews in his Civil War uniform

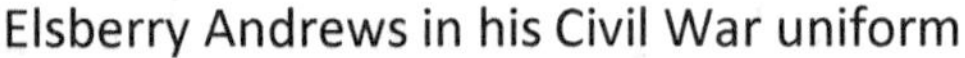

Maybe you don't think you look like your relatives.  These two are generations apart and I think they look alike. What do you think? Pictured left is Elsberry Jackson Andrews (1843-1917). On the right is Jefferson Reid Gladden (1960) son of Mildred (Mit) and Curtis Gladden.  Mit is the youngest of Thomas Reid and Maggie Bryant's children and Jeff is the last grandchild. Elsberry would be Jeff's Great Grandad.  How strange is that. Sometimes you just can't get away from your relatives. One picture was made in the 1860's and one in the 1990's. Years apart but strangely close.

E.J. Andrews was a PVT in Co. 6,7 in the AL Infantry, Confederate States of America, Army.  He is buried in Post Oak Springs Baptist Church Cemetery in AL.

His gravestone reads:  Thou shall be missed because thy seat will be empty.

An older Elsberry Jackson Andrews. The year of the photo is not known.

# The children of

## Hester Homesley Andrews and Elsberry Jackson Andrews

Wiley Madison Andrews- April 19,1868-Sept. 17,1941
Mary Andrews Cobb-August 29,1869-Sept.26,1912
J.A. Andrews-August 6,1870-August 11,1870
John J. Andrews-Sept 8,1871-January 23,1957
Calvin Lawson Andrews-January 26,1874-November 27,1939
Edd Macon Andrews-January 9,1876-May 13,1941
Margaret Marilla Andrews Bryant-Sept. 14,1877-November 1,1953
Barbra Nora Andrews Burgess-February 19,1879-July 5,1910
Sallie J Andrews-February 12,1880-October 22,1953
Thomas Perry Andrews-January 8,1882-April 20,1965

## Lou Gwin Andrews and Elsberry Jackson Andrews

Hester Andrews Owen-September 24,1895-November 29,1968
Bessie Andrews Owen-January 2, 1898-September 12,1970

It is believed that this is Elsberry with Hester or Lou. After Hester died Elsberry married Lou. I am not sure which one is in the picture or which three of their children are pictured. This is one of the unknowns. Another unknown is why Barbra spelled her name Barbra. That is how it is written on her gravestone. Actually, the spelling makes her different.

**Some photographs of the Children and Grandchildren of**

**Elsberry Andrews and Hester Homesley Andrews**

**and Elsberry and Lou Gwin Andrews**

This is Willie Andrews. He is the son of Wiley Andrews (April 19,1868-Sepember 17,1941) which was the first born of Elsberry and Hester Andrews.  Wiley is Maggie Bryant's brother.  Willie would be the grandchild of Elsberry and Hester Andrews.

Even though the picture is not as good as some, this is one of the oldest photos in the collection.  It is a tintype photo of Lawson Andrews who they all called Uncle Loss. Tintype photos were used in the 1800's so it has been around a while. Loss is Maggie Bryant's brother and he was close to Maggie and Thomas Reid. They eventually bought their house in Jacksonville from him, remodeled it and lived in it from 1918 until their death. Loss eventually went to live in Mississippi along with a lot of the other relatives.

More Andrews side of the family photos are included here.  This one has written on the photo Uncle Loss and his railroad gang. It is believed that he is the one holding the fiddle in the center of the gang. Calvin Lawson (Loss) was the fifth born child to Elsberry Jackson Andrews and Hester Andrews. He lived January 26,1874-November 27,1939.

He and most of the Andrews brothers went to Mississippi for railroad work or to farm according to the census records. Some are buried in Mississippi, but some returned to Alabama later in life and are buried in Alabama. Loss, his wife and some of their children are buried in Post Oak Springs Cemetery in Jacksonville, Alabama.

On the back of this photo is written Uncle Loss and Aunt Pet Andrews. Once again, this would be one of Maggie Andrews Bryant's brothers and his wife whose name was Willie Bell but they called her Pet? That must be some story that goes with that. They look so happy in the photo.

This is the Calvin Lawson (Loss) Andrews family in front of their home? It is scary how similar it is to the Bryant house in Alabama. We think it might have been taken at the home place In Alabama before the house was remodeled? No one is around to tell us if that is true or if this is their home in Mississippi. Some things we just have to guess about. You compare the photos and decide what you think.

Front row L-R: Vera, Loss, Pet, Coy. Back row includes Coot, Ina, and Claud. At least that is what is written on the back of the photo.

The photo on the left is Sam Johnson and his wife Nora Andrews
Johnson. The outfit is wonderful.  She is Lawson and Pet Andrew's daughter and
only lived till she was 25. At this time, the details of her death are not known.
She is buried at Post Oak Springs Baptist Church Cememtery  and a portion of
his picture is on the tombstone. Her tombstone reads: She was too good, too
gentle and fair, to dwell in this cold world on earth.  I would love to know more
about her.

The photo booth photos on the right are of Bessie and Hester Andrews.
They are the youngest of the Elsberry Andrews children.  It looks like a fun day.
I would love to know the story behind those photos. They would  later marry
Owen brothers and move to Mississippi to raise their families.

Years later after the photo booth shots of Bessie were taken, here she is with her husband Hardy and their children in Mississippi. Bessie is Maggie Bryant's sister, so these are nieces and nephews to Maggie. Pictured is Bessie, Merle, Hardy, Gene, Mildred peaking over his shoulder and Buie. These are all their children except Juanita who died before her first birthday.  She is buried at Corinth Cemetery in Lumberton, Mississippi. So is Lou Andrews, Bessie's Mom, who was Elsberry Andrews second wife. Bessie is the youngest of Elsberry's children.

This is Lois, Buie and Faye Owen in the bottom left photo.  On the right, is Merle Owen with her niece Faye.  Both Buie and Merle are the children of Bessie Andrews Owen and Thaddeus Aaron Owen who they called Hardy.

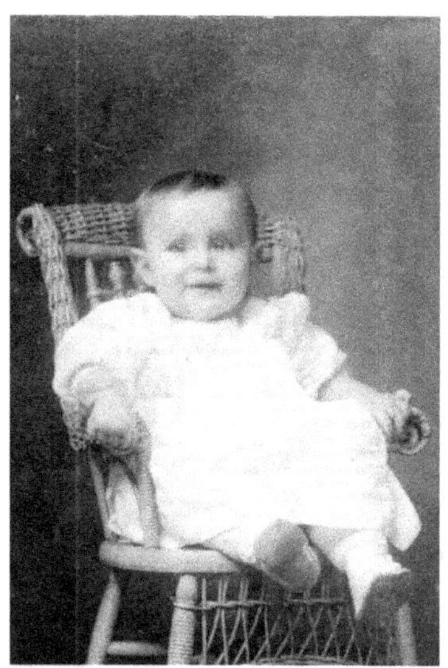

Here is Barbra Andrews Burgess and her children. This is Maggie's sister. One is Josh and the other is believed to be Nannie. Barbra was born just after Maggie in 1879. She lived February 19,1879-July 5, 1910. She and her husband John were married in 1903. She did not live long after their marriage. Please note that this is how her name is spelled on her tombstone so it is not a typo. She and John are buried in the Union United Methodist Church Cemetery in Wellington, Alabama.

This is Edd Macon Andrews and his family.  This would have been Margaret's Brother. They lived in Mississippi along with Hester Andrews Owen and Bessie Andrews Owen who are he and Maggie's sisters. In the 1920 census, Edd and Margaret (his wife) are listed as having 11 children. I am not sure who is shown here but I think it is Lawson, Jack, Greene, Leoma and Robert. They later had Elmer, Elzie, Annie, Hugh, Nellie, and James by the 1920 census count.  Edd, his wife and some of their children are buried in Wake Forest Cemetery in Mississippi.

The Owen Family-Allen Owen, Jack Owen, Lisa Owen and Hester Andrews Owen. Hester Andrews Owen is Maggie Andrews Bryant's sister. Hester and Bessie Andrews married brothers and lived in Mississippi. There was also a Lee Owen that lived beside them in Mississippi. His wife's family was from Mississippi and maybe that is why they all moved there. Some say it is because they worked for the railroad. We may never know.

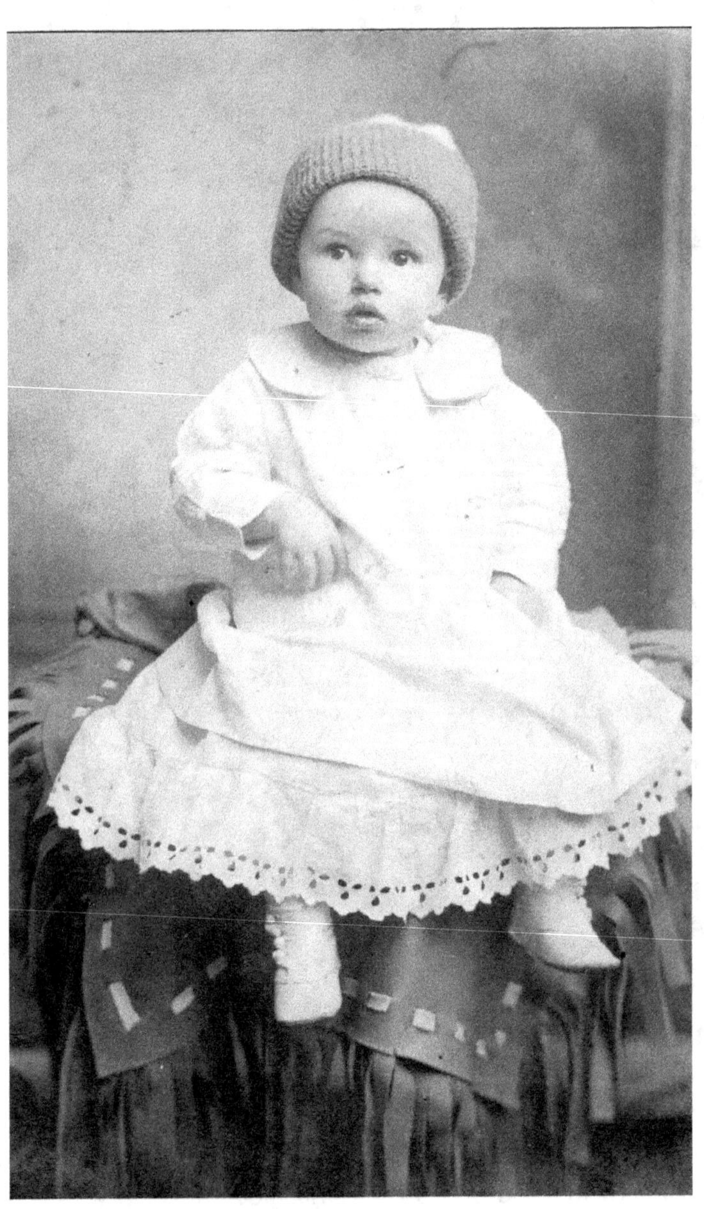

This is Jack Owen as a baby. He is Hester Andrews Owen and Allen Owen's son. I think because they lived in Mississippi they sent lots of pictures to Alabama so everyone could keep up with all the children. I am glad because that is why we have them now.

This is Edith Mae Owen, she Is Allen and Hester Andrews Owen daughter.  She was born in 1920 so can you guess her age?

Here are the siblings of Maggie Bryant plus a few others. In the front row is Sallie Andrews, Lillie Gray her niece, Pet (Loss' wife). On the back row are Loss Andrews, Maggie Bryant, Tom Andrews and Sallie Andrews (Tom's wife). In the photo below are siblings to Maggie L-R: Loss Andrews, Sallie Andrews, Maggie Bryant, and Thomas Andrews.

Below left is a picture of Lawson and Wiley Andrews. In the middle photo is John Andrews. All of these are siblings to Maggie Bryant. Some are buried in Post Oak Springs Baptist Church Cemetery. Some stayed in Mississippi and are buried there. On the top right is Jack Andrews, Edd Macon Andrews son.  The bottom photo did not have any names but I think that they are Andrews? We know Maggie Bryant is the second in line in the photo and the others are either siblings or sister in-laws.

I have a few pictures during the in between years. Here is Maggie in 1937 and then again with Tom and Sallie Andrews the same day. Below is Mildred who they called Mit along with Maggie Bryant on a trip to St. Augustine. They meet up with Edd there in the photo below. It is believed Edd did his service training not far from St. Augustine in Camp Blanding in Florida.

Here is Mildred in front of a car in 1941 and Mit again with Homer and Orwell.  We think that one was her boyfriend at the time but she is not here for us to ask. That is how rumors get started.

Thomas Reid and Maggie in front of the home place on the left and Maggie showing off her new stove in the bottom right photo. That was the best stove of the day.  I am sure she had reason to show it off.

The top left is Mildred Bryant and her friend, Geneva Page.  On the top right, it looks like just a Sunday on the porch. Today it was Bama, Mildred, Elzora, Sallie and Maggie on the porch.  The question is how does Bama fit into the family. Research is ongoing.  Below is Elzora and Bob Wynn on the left. Edd Bryant looks like he is having a rest in the photo on the right.

**Children and Grandchildren of Thomas Reid and Maggie Andrews Bryant**

1.  Ethel and Cleve Fite
    Children-Ruth (1922-2011) and Helen (1931-2009)
2.  Andrew and Nannie Bryant
    Child-Harlan (1922-2001)
3.  Elzora and Robert Wynn
    Children- Margaret (1924-1986), Howard (1927-1976) and
    Bobby Ralph (1932)
4.  Anna Mae and Ed Moore
    Children-Edna (1925-2006), Haskell (1927-2003), William
    Norman (1929- 1933), Marlene (1931-2014) and Barbara
5.  Thomas Reid Bryant Jr. (1905-1907)
6.  Renfroe and Annie Bryant
    Children-Morris (1928-1929), Edith Mae (1930), Faye, Arlene,
    Johnny Reid, Charles, Duane (1941-2008), Ernie (1944-1990),
    Donald, and Mickey
7.  Velma Odell Bryant (1909-1910)
8.  Clarence and Robbie Bryant
    Children-Billy, Melda and Donnie (1949-1968)
9.  Ralph and Mildred Bryant
    Children-Thomas, Eckols and Lowell
    Ralph and Stella
    Children-Ralph Jr.
    Ralph and Ann
    Children-David and Brenda (1946-1952)
10. Edd and Gwinell Bryant
    Child-Belita (1948-2011)
11. Mildred and Curtis Gladden
    Children-Terry, Anita, Coleman (1956-2002) and Jefferson

Below is a picture of an unhappy Johnny Reid Bryant that starts off our T.R. and Maggie Bryant Grandchildren photos.

Now we will start with the grandchildren of Thomas Reid and Maggie Bryant. Oh, how they were photographed. Here are a few pictures we found in the collection. We start with Ethel and Ruth in the top photo.  Ethel Bryant Fite was the first born and the first to have a grandchild. The photo on the lower right is Margaret Wynn who is the daughter of Elzora and Robert Wynn.  Then on the left is Ruth Fite again a few years older.

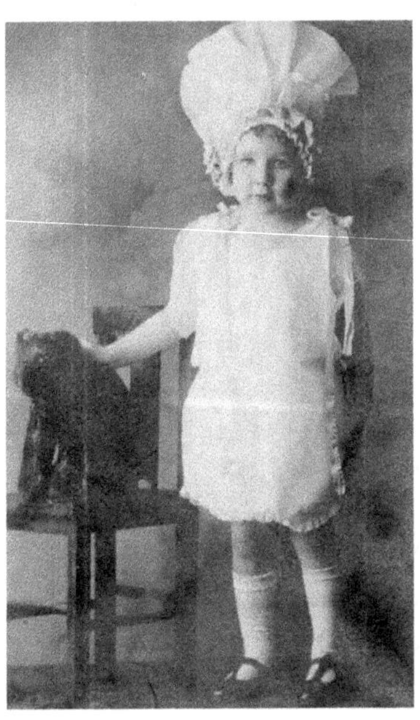

The top photo is Anita and Terry Gladden, children of Mildred and Curtis Gladden. The photos on the bottom are Ruth and Helen, just a few years later in the different pictures.  They grow up fast.

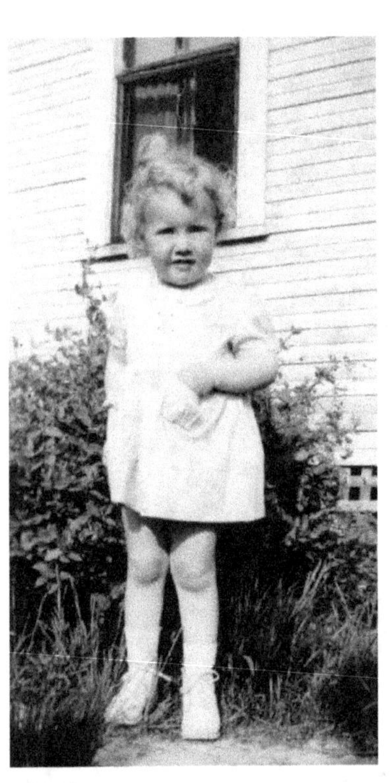

The photo on the left is Melda, daughter of Clarence and Robbie Bryant. The photo on the right is Billy and Johnny Reid. It must be new overall day.  Billy is the son of Clarence and Robbie also. Johnny Reid is the son of Renfroe and Annie Bryant.

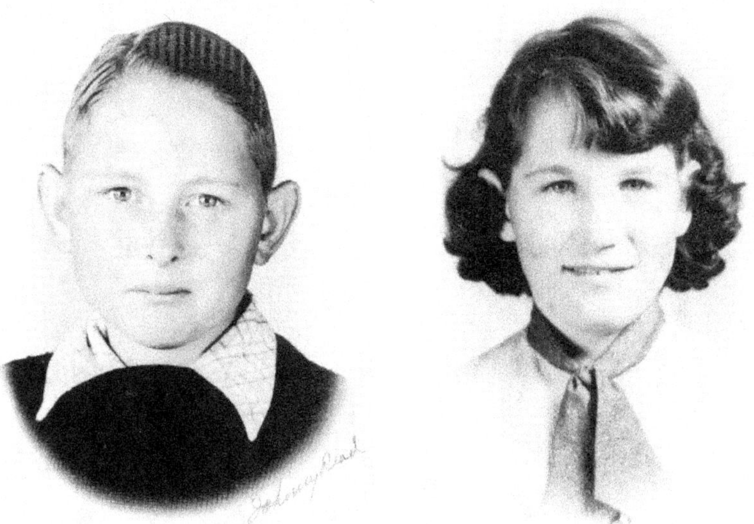

In the top photo are two of the Gladden boys, Jeff and Coleman, they are the sons of Mildred and Curtis Gladden. They are the last grandchildren born to Thomas Reid and Maggie.  In the lower left is Johnny Reid, son of Renfroe and Annie Bryant. The bottom right photo is Anita Gladden, Daughter of Mildred and Curtis Gladden.

These are many photos of the grandchildren that Mit had in her collection. Some are pictured twice. They were just too good not to share. Top: Ruth, Helen, Margaret, Howard 2nd row: Belita, Billy, Melda 3rd Row: Principal Edd Moore, Edna, Marlene, Barbara 4th Row: Edna, Marlene, Haskell and Haskell again. I hope it brings back memories of days gone by.

Top Row: Faye, Faye, Johnny, Ernie 2nd Row: Arlene, Arlene, Arlene, Eckols 3rd Row, Mit age 10 who is not a grandchild but one of the children of T R and Maggie, then Thomas, Thomas and Lowell 4th Row: Anita, Terry, Coleman, and Jeff. If your family didn't share photos with Mit then your picture is not here. Not all of the grandchildren are pictured but this is a lot of them.

In the top photo are some of the granddaughters. We have pictured Helen. Faye, Marlene, Melda, Barbara, and Arlene. In the bottom photo is part of the Renfroe Bryant family. They had ten children. Two died before their first birthday. Pictured here are L-R: Faye, Arlene, Charles, Duane, Johnny, Renfroe, Annie and Ernie probably about 1945.

The next generation is coming up and they keep adding more. On the left is Buddy Boozer (a neighbor and cousin), Thomas, Lowell and Echols. Pictured right is Terry Gladden and T.R. Bryant. Picture below are L-R: Haskell Moore, Howard Wynn, Thomas Bryant, Lowell Bryant, Billy Bryant, Echols Bryant, and Johnny Reid Bryant.

The top photo includes L-R: Arlene, Marlene, Faye, Barbara, Johnny Reid, Billy, Lowell, and Echols. The photo on the bottom has stair steps of children L-R: Helen, Fay, Marlene, Barbara and Arlene.

The names may not be correct but this is what was written on them. The top photo Front L-R: Billy, Echols, Johnny, Lowell. Back L-R: Arlene, Marlene, Faye and Barbara. The bottom photo includes L-R: Johnny Reid, Faye, Charles, Marlene, Barbara, Duane, Helen and Arlene.

Here are the some of the grandsons. The top photo has Lowell, Roberta the dog, Echols, Thomas and a dog named Tig. The dogs and boys looked like they were having fun. The bottom photo has Billy, Lowell, Echols, Johnny, Charles and Ralph Jr.(Tooter).

The top photo is Maggie, Terry Gladden, Thomas Reid Bryant and Mildred Bryant Gladden.  Here is Jefferson Reid Gladden on the left with Thomas Reid. The right bottom photo is Mildred again with her daughter Anita and oldest son Terry when they are a few years older.

Here are more of the grandchildren. Have you counted?  How many do Thomas Reid and Maggie have?  Unless my math is off there are 35 grandchildren born but not all are still living. Some did not make it to adult hood. The family has been blessed with lots of children.  Thomas Reid got to meet all of his grandchildren. Jefferson Reid Gladden was the last to be born in 1960. Sadly, Maggie passed away in November of 1953 so she got to see all but Jeff and his brother, Curtis Coleman Gladden Jr. (1956-2002) both pictured here with him and Viola. This is the only photo we have found of T.R. laughing.

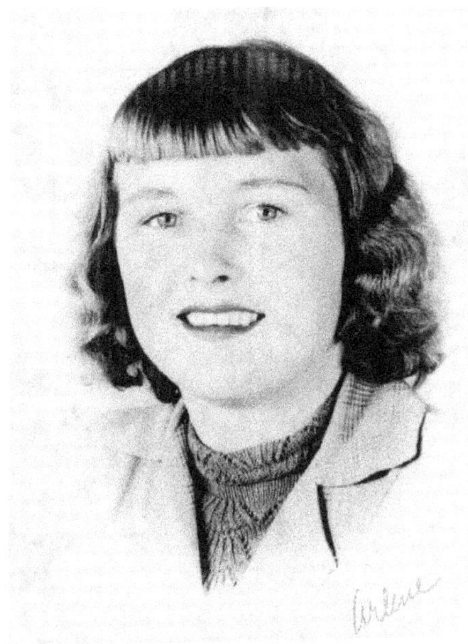

    Here are some of the grandchildren all grown up. The top photo is Ruth and Bill Williams in their wedding photo. Ruth is the daughter of Ethel and Cleve Fite. The top right is Arlene, daughter of Annie and Renfroe Bryant. On the bottom left is Barbara Moore and right is Edna Moore, both daughters of Anna Mae and Ed Moore.

Here are Mildred's (Mit) children in the top left photo. Terry, Anita, Coleman, and Jefferson Gladden. It was cowboy day for the Gladden boys. In the right top photo is the Fite family. L-R: Ruth, Helen, Ethel and Cleve. Below is a picture of Elzora with her children, Howard and Margaret.

Pictured here in the top left photo are Howard and Margaret.  The whole family gets in the picture on the right. Margaret, Bob, Elzora and Howard Wynn.

Like mother, like daughter. Beauty ran in the family here. This is Gwinell Bryant and her daughter Belita Bryant Heathcock. They are wife and daughter to Edwin Bryant better known as Edd.

Here are Cleve and Ethel Fite. Ethel is the first born to T.R. and Maggie Bryant. In the right top photo, Margaret Wynn (Daughter of Elzora and Bob Wynn) is with Thomas Reid and Maggie in front of the house. Below is Mit with her four children. L-R: Anita Smith, Coleman Gladden, Mildred, Jeff Gladden, and Terry Gladden. Mildred lived to be 90 and died in 2011. She was the last born to T.R. and Maggie Bryant and the last to pass away of that generation.

For those that always come to the Bryant Reunion each year, you may remember these faces more than the younger version of them.  Clarence Bryant and his wife Charlotte are in the top left. Top right is Annie and Renfroe Bryant. On the bottom left is Clarence and Mit. The last two siblings to make it to the reunion. Clarence lived from January 2, 1911 – December 13,2003. Mit lived July 28,1920 -April 28, 2011.  On the bottom right is Ralph Bryant Jr. and his wife Virginia. In all the photos, Ralph Jr. is always called "Tooter".

Did you know? Elzora Bryant married Bob Wynn. Renfroe Bryant married Annie Wynn, Bob's sister. This makes their children double first cousins.

We cannot talk about the Bryant Family without talking about the school. Across the street from the Bryant house was Cedar Springs School. Thomas Reid Bryant and his brother in law, Lawson Andrews donated the land in 1920 so that it could be built. Many children went through that school including some of the Bryant children and many years of generations to come.

It went through lots of changes and in 1988 it closed its doors for the last time as a school. The memories still linger of the almost 140 years in the community and the many children passing through those doors. The children would come across the street to the store owned by Thomas and Maggie each afternoon and sometimes even as a field trip to buy snacks and drinks. The store which was there by their home was a thriving part of the community for 50 plus years.

All the children from the school solemnly walked to the house across the street to say goodbye to their lifetime friend when Thomas Reid Bryant died. They all knew him well. He was 93 when he died and not long after his death the store closed.

This was the home place on any Sunday afternoon.  All that was needed were some rockers, a swing and always some sweet tea.  Mildred Bryant, the youngest of Thomas Reid and Maggie's children, painted the old home place as she remembered it so well. She often talked about the days spent there.

When Mildred Bryant told stories of the old home place, the stories of the store were included. She wrote poems and stories about it all before she passed away in 2011. There are a few pictures around but these paintings are testament to how dear these places were to her and her life. Her paintings are in color but here in black and white I think you see the past captured through Mit's eyes. Below is a photograph of the store after it had closed.

**T.R. Bryant General Merchandise Gas and Oil.**

**The Store as everyone called it.**

John Boozer

A poem by John Boozer (a cousin) says it all.

"In that old store, we sat around

And never went home until the sun went down.

Many a meal we did make,

Of a cinnamon roll and a Nehi grape.

I remember quite well, it came a big snow

And the thermometer went to four below.

That was the only time we became disgusted

Everything froze, and the drinks all busted!

Those days are gone, and there will be no more

Settin' around that little country store.

Mildred and her dad, Thomas Reid Bryant, posing for the camera.

She always had stories to tell about her life as a Bryant. After her death, we have found notebooks full of story after story, lots of poems and all kinds of notes. As you can see, she kept lots of photographs for us to discover too. I hope she can see us from Heaven and is smiling at how her collection is being taken care of and shared. She would have loved the book.

# Thomas Reid Bryant and Maggie Andrews Bryant

Just some snap shots of them during their many years together.

This is a photo of Thomas and Maggie on their 50<sup>th</sup> wedding anniversary. They had so many years together and it was time to celebrate. They were married on October 25,1869. They had been married 57 years when Maggie passed away in 1953.

Maggie and Thomas Reid Bryant.

Thomas Reid and Margaret Bryant

This was a day in the life of Thomas Reid Bryant. If you look closely, you can see on the wall the picture included in the book of the photo of his Parents and their 56th Wedding Celebration.  They say it was always about family to them. The hope now is that the new generation keeps that love of family going strong.

On the last pages of the book is a poem written by Mit Bryant. It has included in it everything that you would need to know about the things that meant something to her.  She may have shared it already but it seemed right to add this to the book. She always wanted it published and shared.  Here is a poem by Mildred Bryant Gladden Acray and her thoughts on things.

## MY HOUSE TOO FULL OF THINGS

My house is so full of things.
Too full someone said.
But what shall I do with things I love
Such as my Mama's bed
Where each of eleven of us was born?
Some in summer, others spring, some in winter's morn.
And the old scales that set for years
In Papa's country store.
Fifty-seven years they weighed every baby born
In Cedar Springs and all around
A dozen times or more,
Not to mention all the sugar, beans and cheese.
For heaven's sake don't tell me
I must get rid of these.

Then there's the old embroidery thread case
That I use for a silver chest.
I've sold many a skein of thread from it
Along with all the rest
Of things like handkerchief and ribbons
From the other small showcase,
For which I searched every corner
Until I found a place
Where I could tuck it in.

All the memories that go with those
I must also include
The old nail keg from the store
That I made into a stool,
Remembering with each and every stitch
That went into the cover
The times I 'd snitched three-penny nails
Along with all the other.
Such as empty cigar boxes,
Pap's hammer, saw and awl
To build my fancy blue-bird houses
That I nailed to the smoke house wall.

Now there's the old, old spool case,
A 1900 relic Mama's brother made.
You really don't think, do you,
That I could lay that in the shade?
Why it's just the thing to hold those little gifts
My kids have given me.
The perfect place to keep them out
For everyone to see.

Well, what about that old rocking chair,
The one with the broken back?
That's what Mama started housekeeping with
In 1896 and there's another one that's black.
The first one rocked eleven kids
From the first day they were born,
And when little Thomas Reid got sick
It rocked all night and morn.

For six long weeks, it never stopped
And Mama never slept.
She kept her vigil night and day
And crooned and prayed and wept.
The rockers on this chair
Were completely worn away
Before God took little T.R. home
So how can I ever say
I have no room in my house
For such a love as this?
Of course, there must be some place
That I won't ever miss.

The black rocker? Well, that's another story.
If it could talk, I'm sure that
It would tell a tale of glory.
Of how it came to be a part of all the finery
That was purchase when we began
To board the School Teachers...all three,
Along with the old oak wash stand and
The dresser with the hat box,
The black iron bed, the center table,
Lamp and a new mantel clock.
All these occupied the "front room"
With the parlor organ. Now, now,
There just ain't no way I could part
With these things, anyhow.

How many times that ole' organ
Was played by my three sisters
Before I was even born.
Then when I was seven and
I learned shaped notes and...Heaven!
The Do, Re, Mi's are still with me,
But lines and spaces leave me yearning.
Yet still I love to pump and play
"Let The Lower Lights Be Burning".
So the organ must have a corner
In my house too full of things.
Though my piano may be newer
Somehow it just doesn't bring
The love and all the memories
That can make my heart take wings.
And sing with joy and happiness
In my house so full of things.

There's no telling in the world how many
Heel and sole tacks Pap used
With that old shoe last there
That he kept to half-sole shoes.
You see the seven pound smoothing iron
That sets beside the door
It was used every Tuesday ironing day
For fifty years or more.

And that old gallon syrup jug
There by the hearth side,
We used it for a water jug
When we worked the fields backside,
We set it in the coolest shade
At the end of those long rows and I tell
That water stayed just as cold
As it came from the well.

Oh yes, I must not forget
The twine holder from the store.
It held the twine that wrapped the cheese,
The coffee sacks, and many, many more
Such as over-alls, brogan shoes,
Calico prints and thread.
It surely had to have a place
Just like my Mama's bed.
You ask about the gum machine,
It's not fancy or very bright,
But the school kids dropped their pennies in
With great joy and delight
To receive one…two…or three selections
Of the "Perfection"…Delicious Confection".

Oh, the clock on the mantel
With the gold crane on the door?
They started keeping house with that too.
Need I tell you more?
Except to say that it was with great fascination
I watched Papa every Saturday night
Wind each spring up good and tight
So that it would strike each hour
All through the next long week.
Then we knew just when to get up
And when to go to sleep.

Don't miss that little black table
There beside the door.
That was my sister Ethel's piece
Given to me to keep.
For years it held their radio
That played the girls to sleep.
Then Cleve would listen to the news
Lowell Thomas I believe.
Also Amos 'N' Andy and Lum 'N' Abner;

Now can you really conceive
Of me moving that to some dark place
As a closet or such thing
And never, never know the joy
Of all this remembering?

In this all of the memories
In my house with lots of things?
No, there is one more
That crowds my bedroom floor
I look, and my heart sings.
This is my baby trunk
Bought especially for me
'Cause I'm the last of the eleven,
The baby...don't you see.
The trunk, it held my clothes, my dolls
And all my childhood treasures
For years. Then came the sad day
With heartbreak beyond measure.

The war had come...World War II.
And brother Edd was leaving.
There's no way I can tell you
How the family was a' grieving.
He had to have a foot locker
To carry into camp,
So my baby trunk became his trunk
Until he was shipped out.
He lived through two long years
Of South Pacific combat.
The government returned my trunk.
Now this is where it's at.

Many years have come and gone,
But memories are real today.
All the family now but two
Have quietly slipped away.
When I walk through my crowded house
Of lots of stuff and things.
No decorator here on earth could know
The sweet joy that it all brings
Just to be able to remember
Those happy times gone by
Sometimes with sadness, more often gladness,
But both with tear dimmed eye
For joy in knowing that one day soon
We'll all be together once again
In our home up in the sky.

Thank God for my inheritance,
Not just for my "stuff and things"
But for the love and kindness taught me,
And the joys these virtues bring.
My heart shouts with gratitude;
My soul takes off on wings
As I walk among my memories
In my house "too full of things".

**Mildred Bryant Gladden Acray**
October 1, 1984